dear iris

Manasvini Duggal

BlueRose Publishers
New Delhi • London

First Published in September 2021

ISBN: 978-93-5472-208-0

BLUEROSE PUBLISHERS

www.bluerosepublishers.com

info@bluerosepublishers.com

+91 8882 898 898

Cover Design:

Muskan Sachdeva

Typographic Design:

Ilma Mirza

Distributed by: BlueRose, Amazon, Flipkart

Starlight

Did the thought of this ever feel so lost?

I got a tattoo ingrained where the tears bled loss.

Dripping constellations on a brand new sky,

my colours change, but the thought of you is still alive.

Here's to me, always looking for the "why not" in the "why."

Here's to you, to what you think is our demise.

~*~

Preface

Back in 2019, whilst waist-deep in the pressure of my final year board exams, I remember feverishly going through some of my old poetry from a year or so before. I recall myself rephrasing entire verses and changing their seemingly uneven structures until I realised how much even six months had changed my sense of writing as a poet. Things had changed in the way I saw transience, memories, nostalgia, and so much more. I remember feeling excited because I suddenly felt a need to explore this change concretely- through more words. Now, it has been a year to the culmination of my school-going years. What has followed this new chapter is an exploration into my potential as a poet, an exploration that has sprung from thousands of words, with thousands more yet to come.

Poetry for me has never been an escape. It has never taken the shape of a rabbit hole down which the burdens of the real world suddenly lose their potency. On the contrary, any burden I have come across, I often write about. It is never an act of escape that follows, but rather a step towards letting go. Through my work I allow myself to feel and process my experiences, and the emotions that come with them. In the process, anything I create is an attempt to capture a "coming of age" narrative. I am nineteen right now and on the brink of a decade that allows for new cities, new friends, new loves and above all, entirely new lives. The first of what I hope will be many, this collection of poems has been handpicked from all that I have written in the past year. From initial musings in lockdown to pieces inspired by my first experiences in college, the poems showcase a somewhat chronological pattern of thought. By pouring my mind and heart onto these pages, I hope that the reader too finds a piece of themselves in what I have to say.

Contents

Vintage

10 am, and the morning starts the same,

coffee in a flowery cup,

the burnt sunlight filtering through a window's cusp,

the screens all light up, and the day begins again.

But by 5 pm, the burn softens into a mist,

the clouds collect, hold a canvas erect,

while the watercolours are splashed onto a palette,

pale blue, slight magnolia, a sultry pink

watch as a lilac and orange evening emerges.

At this point, twilight submerges the mind as well,

clarity shifts, or maybe comes into focus again.

In retrospect, maybe I should have left my doubts lie dormant,

the chaos which has followed was not worth the end.

Something so beautiful could have been glamorously vintage,

but that image lies hacked in an attic again.

Manasvini Duggal

First time, second time, seventh, and tenth,

still ready for more of you as yet.

Meanwhile, the watercolours drip,

the comet less ink behind is let slip,

and the day sees its red curtains roll in.

That bloom of colour melts into purgatory again,

and with it,

that which is now vintage

because of all those months of lost control

now comes closer to being an antique instead .

~*~

Aurora

Dozing in the dry daylight,

when the feeling hits slow

the depths of an aurora,

a holy perception of all black and rose-gold;

after dark is when the spirits lie close.

Miss being taken down,

over, across, and around,

where the galaxy rusts

under the shimmer of its deepest dawn.

I miss the feeling I used to get,

the goofy way I overdosed, overspent;

I miss the stupid love songs

that made their way into my rock song-set.

Wide awake in the dipping sunlight,

the feeling would hit hard,

overplay the same scenarios;

perennial restart,

let it loose, as the pinks turn to violet,

violet turns to night.

I'd hate the tears that would flow

free fall as if it was their birth right.

After dark it became a mesmerising taunt,

the constant rose-tipped thorn in my side.

Remember then,

the way I overdosed instead,

on heartbreaks; a hell quantified

on that broken note, that wretched line,

I hate the way those love songs disappeared overnight.

Now, strutting wide-eyed,

staring at that molten November sky,

a river cruising teal; I walk right on by,

time made me bolder, made me realise

all my demons need not have that smile.

Skipping across a nebula

of violet and gold, ink, and carmine.

I miss the feeling you gave me still,

but maybe I just miss your presence in my life.

/after dark is when aurorae erupt in my hindsight/

~*~

Manasvini Duggal

Affair

To be loved, in all totality,

doe drop eyes, hushed little smiles,

a look of submission

and glances adorned so pure and high,

there is no sweeter innocence than in those who fall.

To have felt, in all totality,

the steady rush, slow at first,

then a racy fervour; a single touch,

to feel and understand

what those poets and dreamers,

all those makers of art search for.

But to lose it away

through no fault except yours,

to have the elation once soar,

now become something blatantly small,

insidiously snide,

bitterness is a choice I do not intend to make mine.

So many questions suddenly arise,

what it really means to move on;

is it to forget?

to accept?

to make excuses and hate and deny,

or to remember with the same hushed little smile,

to each their own is how I choose to sleep at night.

Because if all is transactional,

love when loved,

hate when left behind,

then I want no truck with all that's in my mind,

but also to forget, is it to accept?

Or to repress, deny, make up lies?

Is acceptance to love still and walk on,

or let no memory see the light?

To have felt something so profound; now nowhere,

seems impossible to make it likewise an affair,

and yet, others do it with a casualty, of which I am unaware,

tossed in the corner, does it really bother?

is the thought of me too hideous to bear?

because to sink deep; love deep,

leave hate in the shallow end,

all these words I see are beautiful in their despair.

My philosophy, principles in their iron tight atrocity,

why hate or forget at all

when you can subdue

this bitterness from going askew.

Isn't forgiveness such a pretty shade when bare,

to give chances over chances; I never seem to mind,

rather be forgotten than to be the one to leave behind.

To experience, in all its mortality,

the ticking clock on this bond of impracticality,

to move on is neither to forget nor too long,

but maybe live, and let live on.

Even the stars, in February's darkest hours,

seem to shine so bright.

~*~

Pink

Pink was the rose in my hand,

I pictured on its timeless stance,

the aura of paramours, and

the scents that drove them mad

as I thought about the greatest affairs.

Time has nonchalantly forgotten that it had

sunshine on its petals, starburst in my mind

as I longed for that fairytale life,

for the greatest love affairs that I am yet to have.

Pink was the shade of the seashell

I held in a dream I once had.

The waves gently rolled

as a sunset danced upon no land.

Cross-legged I sat, around sisters of pearl

and beads of lapis and lac,

and I thought once more

of that rose so pale, and the sunshine

on its gossamer back.

I thought to myself

of the affairs of a time long past

as the froth of the seas licked my toes.

Thoughts that drown, buried and froze,

daylight dawned, and again I rose.

\\

Would memories of fire

rest as easy as the gods of that sea?

Would clockwork strokes of day and night

flow as fast as my conversations

in a midnight hour of need?

Those human traces that attempt to tear

still do not fray,

would they leave with a whisper,

or with a flourish at the end of their tale

because black comes the stroke

that turns to smoke my state of grace.

Walking fast, edging away

from these hues that hold, fixate their gaze,

miserable comes this haze,

then, I remember ~

//

Dear Iris

Pink were my cheeks,

When I first heard that music box play,

lamplight shaded, alone with our slates

wiped clean, not yet unfrayed,

never saw it coming, hope I see it again,

left me thinking to myself,

if that really was a timeless tale,

or a dream-like wave crashing over my senses.

And now,

pink again is the rose

draped against a worn white wall,

the sunshine still as romanticised.

All that's changed is my state of mind

as I think again, of time in all its incompetence

still, the stars burst as ever before,

as I take in the scent of all those drunk paramours,

and while my camera clicks that fairytale scene,

pink turns the sun, and its lustre colours my cheeks...

~*~

Manasvini Duggal

Drops

My palm, as it rests, senses something wet,

overturned, I see the page it lay on,

smudged words on its edge,

no matter now, cut it straight,

and continue to write as before.

Three seconds later, maybe five,

notice ink trickling down from the top left side,

black ink, now purple

and blue in teal,

tiny bit drips down with zeal

over the words I write for you and me.

But this is a memory

from three or two months ago,

it flickers, falters, and leaves

as I come back dazed

to the present, I try to live for.

It's been a while since I last wrote for you,

hand over ink, as the day turns

from sky to gold,

clouds come and change the golden hue,

I realise it's been days since

I last wrote for you.

Because now, again, I write for myself

I write for the moons and that single star

I write for the cosmic revelation;

to the madmen and the truths they scream of.

I write free; braver, and unbridled,

verses after verses of all I think divine,

my soul; the essence for all I wage war,

now screams quieter, for you at night.

Because the drops that fell

over my pages then,

I hated because they were hopelessly absolute in their fall,

but the drops that flow now,

rain and hope that crashes from the skies that allow.

I welcome the letters they erase as they trickle on down.

Drops of water; astute, profound,

remnants of the millennia they leave behind,

but drops that tear; making me stark and bare.

I know passed has the time,

where they, in all their solitary fright,

wreaked havoc over the lines

through torture is born the golden hour,

but the agony only wastes all its shine.

Though you are mentioned,

it is not for you that I write.

My palm rests, over the palest satin;

the euphoria of what I do now rest in my mind.

Three seconds later, maybe five,

I look to see the molten gold drip, with its silver lines.

I feel the raindrops embedded in my face;

my strands, my soul, my spine.

I smile now as they trickle down,

down the page,

down the same top left side.

~*~

Wild-eyed

Wild eyes, on a spirit, running slow,

autumn lies brisk as red leaves brush

against the evergreen that flows.

Words left unsaid; lyrics fill the spaces left blank.

Thoughts from the past, long gone numb

as the city lights take over,

fill in the senses once deaf and dumb.

Feel so alive;

wild-eyed as a spirit flies high,

the buildings above soar,

as the sunlight bathes them in a rose-pink shine,

decaying stone; gold lit skies,

a city full of devils, of angels drifting dead in the night.

Think of new homes as the landscapes flee right by,

all alone, legs propped up high

outside the pale pink breaks,

rays glimmer through the softest rain;

the rain turns into midnight.

Manasvini Duggal

Lost myself

in the midst of a heartbeat, I cannot define.

Found myself too;

wild-eyed,

under the lasting lore of these horizon-less skies.

Once again, I romanticise

the cobbled streets; the fairy-lit signs,

spending nights, intoxicated,

screaming revolution at the top of my voice.

Once again, I realise

being complete is easiest felt,

hardest to have left behind.

Wild-eyed, on a 1 a.m. night,

a slow-paced stroll,

when I remember to realise

all my demons, they still have your smile;

a city for the young,

for mistakes and memories so futile,

streets made only to scream revolution

in the dead of night.

Walking home alone,

the leaves crunching beneath my stroll,

I stop to look straight up high,

the last words of a setting star;

the days glow pink in the night,

wild-eyed, stares stay lingering

on a horizon, I am yet to call mine.

Drawing closer, over these streets, I know,

just as well as my mind,

my demons stay faithful in your eyes;

my spirits thrive on this heartbeat undefined. //

~*~

Manasvini Duggal

Conversation Piece

Never thought that I'd like

this coffee crème dipped in carmine,

the splash of maggots

in that gossamer rose,

the glow of fuchsia against the violet wine;

watch it sweep me away,

the lull of wildflowers in a red teal sky,

how they whisper their goodbyes

to all the firsts they've left behind.

Never thought I'd have to wonder

what they thought of my million sides,

watch as I change, over and again,

another dozen times

undefined;

finally love myself, even unrefined.

~ Won't you come along my way;

this dash of complication in my lilac skies.

Am I still your conversation piece,

do I still fuel that hoax you feed your mind? ~

But wallflowers wither,

and suns still rise over their faded dye,

"Don't let me go, stay with me still",

I care less and less as the days go by

because only now I realise-

made the wrong things my constant,

when I should've been my own,

been my own mistake,

but now I'm learning to forgo.

//

Breathe in the scent

of jasmines and coconut oil.

Who would have thought I'd embrace

my wildest and my calm

at the same exact time.

Did not think I could break this way,

could push myself to be alright.

Never thought I'd like to see

autumn leaves on my cuffed jeans,

rain washed hair and the harshest breeze,

the lull of everything new,

I still need to love about me;

vintage reels under that one headlight.

I am what I need

to rediscover, realign.

~

A cold that soaks

right through your thighs,

big black boots,

rainbows that tattoo my vice,

purple lips, decadent eyes,

never thought I'd happen to find

this landslide that makes it all alright.

~*~

Doubt

I. Mirror my reflections, mirror that smile,

vanity shades what is felt inside,

doubt I need someone around; slowly that doubt resigns,

been drawing blanks in the aftermath of all that's left behind,

doubts flood over, like tidal waves on mars.

Who knew your words lasted even shooting stars?

ii. Mirror those actions, mirror your life,

I doubt I will circle these drains for the last time.

What started a tragedy, a trademark modern fatality,

is now an anthology of everything deemed juvenile,

doubt that presence will ever wander back home in time,

doubt its absence will ever vacate for another life.

iii. Feel different, as I etch my words upon weathered tiles,

I still see polished stone stretching for miles,

A sole moon reflected below its dappled moonlight.

I look at myself, question my entirety from a past life,

doubt I need to consume something beyond this moonshine,

feel like saturnalias cascade around me, like cosmic landslides,

turn out the lights, now, it's just me, myself, and I,

 feel like happiness was written for me, doubt it's ever beyond sight.

~*~

Hope

"Hope is the thing with feathers,"

they say.

Feathers that take flight at man's crimson dawn,

regale themselves through the touch

of lives sprung by angels' spawn,

feathers that call for a flight

of freedom from the depths of plight;

freedom is the thing that delivers beyond war.

Hope is the thing with errors;

optimism breeds the pride that brings the fall,

but hope is the thing that mirrors,

mirrors the love that messiahs recall.

It is the lonely moment before a heart beats in kind,

errors follow the bold, but fortune follows the sublime.

Hope lies in the hands of scribes,

the touch of whom ignites

fires that burn to rewrite

histories of losses and love; of peace and death,

folklore of immortals that live to be read,

hope births stories that rewind the folds of time;

narratives belong to the bold,

hope belongs to those

favoured by the cusp of all that is divine.

Hope is a fickle love that sways from side to side,

errors engage lovers, as scribes ink their lives.

Hope can be wrong, can be weak and small,

wars aren't always won; lives are always lost,

but at the end of daybreak, in the small of the night,

hope is the stuff of rebellions,

hope is what forces fortune to pick its side,

hope is the thing that brings

humanity out from the depths of hades' shrine,

hope is the thing with feathers

that makes its way across dawn's pink light,

and as I live and breathe,

I see it thrive under the gaze of history's eyes.

~*~

Gaea

Paint for yourself a fickle mountainside

with a sole blue moon against a dappled purple sky,

feel for yourself the rush that begets

a sea of calm against the roar of city lights,

nothing belongs in the world of the benign,

nothing but the breeze that rushes

to trace the edges of that rugged mountainside.

Paint for yourself a pale dawn light,

and the broken birdsong it ushers

as the moon clears itself from white,

think for yourself, the last time you thought

how beauty belongs to the sole blue sky;

to the shifting tides of colours that pass by every night,

surreal to behold, but forgotten on the side

drowned under the ocean of landscapes ruined

by concrete giants above concrete hearts and eyes.

Hear for yourself as the hallowed men sing,

calling out to humankind for their collective myopic sins,

listen for yourself as the madman screams

for those who had long forsaken this hollow land,

and its cursed hollow streams,

fear not though, because blessed are the blameless

and holy are the blind,

the ones who refuse to adhere to the rules,

the laws set before humanity's stake in time.

Sense for yourself, how quiet it is

beyond the putrid stench of a million synthetic arts,

see for yourself, how barren it is;

the edges of that far away mountain and its crumbling parts,

look for yourself,

at those crushed yellow feathers

under darkened soles and lives,

broken pink stems over dark red dyes,

and out there all alone,

a sole white bloom

against the military sky.

Does it stand for hope, for the dawn of faith?

Will you let it snuff out,

a bygone wisp of ignorance and hate.

Paint for yourself a world,

where the monochrome is all that meets the eye,

feel for yourself, an emptiness

as the breeze rushes by that broken mountainside.

~*~

Manasvini Duggal

Dawn

Suns rise every day,

but only over those,

who will themselves

to catch the glow,

break the legions, traverse the flow,

those who dare to be optimists ,

while the herds flock

under the dusk and her shadows.

Sun rises every day,

above what the populace deems hollow,

above where the styxes stray,

where you and the dusks you crave

meet single-file,

where worlds collide,

where the collisions give birth to a single swallow,

the swallow flies straight ahead,

out of breath, out of sight

as the dusk too begs to follow.

Sun rises every day

as the collisions you see

are what you leave behind;

a glorious mess dappled with flickers so slight,

flickers your smiles always reflect, always ignite.

Sun rises as you dream

of all that is there to chase after,

of all the stars that are left

for you to hold onto tight.

Sun rises every day,

and every day, soak through the earth's core,

even so,

all I see are suns that are gone,

oils and acrylics that crack and fade;

it has been a while since I've written about the dawn.

Sun rises every day,

beg to notice everything beyond the fall,

and as each day passes, as sun sets and rise, and soars

I still feel closest to when it's set.

I still wait to fall in love with the dawn.

~*~

Manasvini Duggal

Hold On

Hold onto the memories,

floating alone in the dead of night,

watch as they make you smile so sad,

your lips curl,

as your thoughts swirl mad,

watch them watch over you, in the dead of night.

Hold onto the memories,

as they wipe that tainted slate clean,

as they live and let live,

as they die while you pass through the wrinkles of your life.

Will they wash away from your conscious's shore,

or will you let them live?

As paradise-bound, you move on.

Hold onto the memories,

even though it is cemeteries they hold as shrines,

even though long gone are woes, and long is happiness,

no longer fit into the pieces of your mind,

cemeteries are meant to be remembered,

recalled and revisited, only to let your present being thrive.

Hold onto the memories,

both the beloved and the sins,

onto all the gods, and all the lucifers within,

because roses can bloom

in the depths of December's demise,

because jars full of fireflies

keep you safe even in the crevices of the night.

Hold onto the memories,

your favourite picture

of a flawless winter sky;

even as they make you cry.

Hold onto the memories,

and they will hold onto you.

~*~

Manasvini Duggal

Blush

Sincerity never shies from obscurity,

it seems

it begs to be foretold,

to belong to the centre of the threshold,

between love and a pit of lies.

// Bring me dead flowers,

and I receive them with dead eyes.

To think there is more to a self

than a need to be told that

a love without them is deprived,

to think there is a world out there

that understands

the universe comes and goes at your demise,

to think that love comes with no hurt,

and to escape that hurt is to survive,

what is fundamental to you is worth a lot less

 in my line of sight.

Smoke fills within these eyes,

blooming roses where irises bloom otherwise,

Aphrodite's little January toy,

saw you in a dream; saw you once,

and then another twenty times,

and the sincerity rings true every single time,

break off; break-in; break the soul in line,

hear Aphrodite's cackle as you set your eyes upon mine.

Blush a pale, sweet red,

every midnight without a thought,

watch rationales slumber under a shrouded pall,

it is when adoration that grips the soul,

that every star in the night becomes a waterfall.

Will you pick to be astute, or will you pick the dead end with the red brick wall?

// Choose to hear soft, dappled words,

and a blush that blazes through the doubts.

~*~

Manasvini Duggal

Tokyo

Would you take me home,

to your ginger speckled sky,

where magpies trail behind our magnum opera,

where there are evangelists and Sufis,

and lions riding saffron tides.

Do you think we too can indefinitely thrive?

Would you take me home,

if I say, I want that soft speckled sky?

In love with vampires;

like you, I chase that crescendo in the night,

do my heels screech across this piece?

Does it not harmonise with your ghettoised smile?

In hell with your grandeur,

I see you burn our magnum opera,

now it is not the walls you seek,

but the vines over our grave, climbing high.

Dear Iris

Here comes the sun now,
lilac and scarlet, just another tequila-like rise,
there goes all hope,
as colours splash upon that ginger sky,
forget our home, where we thought worlds ceased to collide,
all I want is the cityscape that crumbles,
where atom bombs and fragile black swans thrive alongside,
where your ghettoised smiles become ghostly
in their ever so depraved plight.

Send me dead flowers, and I will send lavenders wrapped in
twine,
Crushed baby's breath and bloody petalled rose vines.
I miss you,
and I hope you miss my smile,
but the cityscape crumbles, buries me beneath its
chandeliered sky.
Am I right to think this way, to think that home is by your
side?
because Tokyo towers and speckled Tokyo skies,

they really are enough to suffice,
enough to touch and feel and hold onto tight.
//
And yet,
I still wish you held onto my smile.

~*~

Iris

Dear Iris,

I know it is tiring for you to be mine,

believe me, I'm tired too,

I know you fight every day

to hold and to love and just to stay,

I know you question our worth,

our happiness against yours, you weigh,

I see that I win,

but I can feel you sink every time I survive.

"It's not about you, I hope you don't mind."

No, I'm not in the mood to fight tonight.

Dear Iris,

why is it that

those gardenias you bought smell of regret?

Why do they seem to look black

as you kiss me with your sour breath,

screaming silently, "let me go."

You think I don't hear it,

but I understand you so much better than you will never know.

"I need to sleep early, I'll talk to you tomorrow, alright?"

No, I don't think we're breaking up tonight.

Dear Iris,

I saw the way you lusted tonight,

the way you thrusted and pushed and pinned me upright,

I felt the deprivation,

the primordial call of touch starved desperation,

can we make all of it hurt less?

I claw my nails into you as I beg,

we both see the glaring truth that I know turns crystal in our sight,

I call out your name as ecstasy pushes that thought behind.

"You don't doubt that I'll love you forever, right?"

No, I think forever may just be the way we are tonight.

Oh! Iris,

I fought alongside you,

even as I saw the weights shift to your side,

the harder I swam,

the faster the stars seemed to collide,

I know it's over, I heard you give up before your generals could decide,

now I scream silently, "please don't go."

You hear me and crush those gardenias I thought would survive,

our rented home, forever was only, until I turned off the lights,

I see you peer through the chandeliers I left flickering inside.

"Please don't forget me and the things we did, alright?"

No, Iris, I'm still perfectly in love with you tonight.

~*~

Apricity

i. Did the winter sun ever feel so warm

because all I remember are shivering cold shrouds,

little gray swans in little gray clouds.

I remember sunshine peeking out as the swans took flight,

it's new, this feeling,

golden, pink, and sublime,

it's odd seeing the November sky bloom this bright.

ii. I watch someone set the hearth on fire;

the flames burn black, I see them sneak onto their orange
wire,

lying in the wreckage, a half-charred treasure map,

dreams unto dreams, I sit up again and watch time relapse;

the last time I held your hand in my grasp,

the colours fade, and I remember to realise

I miss you, I miss our sunlit speckled smiles,

I miss how freeing the winter felt

as I mourned our demise.

iii. Vintage love stays engrained

in the apricity of a tired sun with tired smiles,

why hasn't December ever felt this pink,

I think.

Well, maybe I never looked beyond the sky,

maybe somethings are meant to be remembered

only under apricated whispers and a muted dye.

~*~

Faith Healer

I still remember that august sun stared me down,

ignite the fall, till dusty brown leaves turned to gold, the ground

uncertainty swept under a flaming rose pink tide,

purity aflame, I cannot forget its starlit shine.

I still remember the December sky with its single cloud,

the way I knew that the preachers could rest,

with what I had found,

the future grew wings as I gradually realised,

that this is how I wish to love, for the rest of this life.

Why feel that handheld gaze under laughter so benign?

the interlaced love-filled strokes

before these courses were set to align,

the best days of life,

suddenly happiness that bites in the dead of night;

circle the drain again, like a million and one other times.

Oh, faith healer,

what else but to turn

to spirits that converse

in the language of the universe, and its free mind

desperately beg for interpretations,

for subtle bars in a love-lorn rhyme

because I still recall may's evenings

and June blue skies.

The last time we heard of the romantics I loved

before they disappeared within the blink of an eye.

Perhaps the same crossroads appeared to two souls that night,

they went one way, and I went mine.

If only we didn't twist our hearts;

villainise the archangels that completed our life.

Redemption comes from the romantics;

the healers, the messengers, the fanatics,

who converse with the world and its gold traced lies.

The past is just a story; recall it however you like,

but what you remember is what saves you;

and I intend to be hurt,

if it means remembering what went right.

Oh, faith healer,

paint for yourself a scene of yellow, gold, and white,

help me retrace the moon's own trails,

and reset the stars that had aligned

my guardian angel, if only I knew

which steps I take are right.

Oh, faith healer,

will you give me back my future

if I ask for it again tonight?

~*~

Acknowledgements

I would like to start by thanking my family- my mother, father, and aunt for constantly urging me to write and exhibit my work. From helping me create and maintain my first blog, to constantly advertising my work and building my confidence, they have been very important to my foundation as a writer. Secondly, thanks to everyone in my team at BlueRose, without whom it would not have been possible to publish this collection. I would also like to extend a special thanks to my dear aunt, Sangeeta mausi, and our dear family friend, Urvashi aunty for their help in designing this cover page with me. Lastly, I would like to highlight the enormous amount of help my closest friends- Aanya, Ananya, Divyanshi, Ishaan, Mehek, Mehul, and Sarah, have been in the process of my writing. From reading every single piece I have ever written, attending my open mics, and keeping me going with their feedback, I know they will be my support system till the end.